Understan VAT

in a week

Philip McNeill and
Sarah Howarth

Headway · Hodder & Stoughton

British Library Cataloguing in Publication Data

A catalogue for this title is available from
the British Library

ISBN 0 340 62102 8

First published 1995
Impression number   10   9   8   7   6   5   4   3   2   1
Year   1999   1998   1997   1996   1995

Typeset by Multiplex Techniques Ltd, St Mary Cray, Kent.
Printed in Great Britain for Hodder & Stoughton Educational,
a division of Hodder Headline Plc, 338 Euston Road, London
NW1 3BH by St Edmundsbury Press, Bury St Edmunds.

the Institute
of Management
FOUNDATION

The Institute of Management (IM) is at the forefront of management development and best management practice. The Institute embraces all levels of management from students to chief executives. It provides a unique portfolio of services for all managers, enabling them to develop skills and achieve management excellence.

For information on the benefits of membership, please contact:

Department HS
Institute of Management
Cottingham Road
Corby
Northants NN17 1TT

Tel: 0536 204222
Fax: 0536 201651

This series is commissioned by the Institute of Management Foundation.

C O N T E N T S

Anyone who manages a business may have to get involved with VAT. That can be a big worry. The VATman expects businesses to act as unpaid tax collectors – and above all, he expects them to get it right. Ignorance of the rules is no defence, and there are financial penalties for those who get it wrong.

Anyone can get to grips with the basic rules of VAT, which means no more worry, plus the confidence to deal with the experts when we meet them.

These are the basic VAT building blocks we will look at:

- VAT categories – tell us what VAT to pay, and when to pay it
- Registration details – tell us when to register or deregister for VAT
- Working out payments and refunds
- Paperwork – what to keep, what to look for
- Schemes and exceptions – tell us when the basic rules get changed
- VAT in Europe
- Relations with the VATman – how to keep on the right track with VAT returns and inspection visits

What is VAT?

VAT is everybody's business. We all pay it. Today we'll start
to get a grip on VAT. We'll take a look at what sort of tax it
is, and what it's meant to do. Then we'll look at the VAT
cycle.

The first steps in the VAT cycle are all about paying VAT:
knowing what is paid and when to pay it.

- Beyond VAT
- VAT at zero per cent
- Paying VAT
- Getting VAT back

VAT spells Value Added Tax. Like any other tax, it ends up
in the government's pocket, but it gets there by a tortuous
route. It flows backwards and forwards between customers,
businesses and VAT men in a cycle that makes Spaghetti
Junction look like a good, straight Roman road. Sometimes it
looks as though it will never get there, but in the end, the
consumer always pays. VAT is a tax on spending. It is aimed
at consumers, not businesses. It is collected by businesses
and overseen by Customs and Excise.

Beyond VAT

To key into VAT, we need to understand the VAT cycle. To
do this, we need to look at the building blocks of VAT.
There are three main categories:

- Spending which is outside the scope of VAT
- Spending which is taxable, but is currently taxed at zero per cent
- Spending taxed at a positive rate of 17.5 per cent or 8 per cent

We shall now look at each of these categories in turn.

Any items we buy that are outside the scope of VAT are called exempt supplies. They include a wide range of items, from insurance and education to postal services and finance.

Exempt supplies might look alluring. Something on which there is no tax sounds like a good deal; but there's a catch.

We can look at exempt supplies from two points of view: as a business or as a member of the public, and either way, snags can arise.

If you are a business, and what you sell is outside the scope of VAT, the snag is this: VAT rules stop you reclaiming any

VAT you have paid out in order to make your sales. If you are a consumer, the snag is this: you may find that the tax-free deal was only a tax-added deal in disguise. The price of your exempt supply might have included VAT after all: hidden VAT. Why? Because the business supplying you couldn't reclaim the VAT it had paid in order to make the sale.

So what goods and services are exempt, and how do we find out?

The VAT authorities don't allow for errors. There is a list – and a golden rule. The rule is – everything is taxable – unless it is included in the list of exemptions set out in the VAT legislation. The list pigeon-holes everything from postal packets to gaming machines, from houseboats to welfare services.

The key to safety lies in remembering that there are no blanket exemptions. Without an exemption, everything is taxable. Alert to the question of exemption, we can be on our guard. We can sum up the points to watch for like this:

Thinking exempt:
- Exempt supplies are specifically listed
- No catch-all exemptions
- When making exempt supplies, no VAT on purchases can be claimed back
- If it's not exempt, it's taxable

Items which are exempt from VAT are as follows:

- Land
- Insurance
- Postal services
- Betting, gaming and lotteries
- Finance
- Education
- Health and welfare
- Burial and cremation
- Trade unions and professional bodies
- Sports competitions
- Works of art
- Some fund-raising activities by charities

VAT at zero per cent

Now we know that exempt supplies can pose dangers to business. So we can begin to appreciate why they welcome VAT at zero per cent. This is the businessman's paradise. No tax is added on to sales, so the consumer is happy, and the business can reclaim from the VATman any VAT it has paid in making the sale, so the business is happy. It is a life of continuous refunds. It also helps to keep sales prices as low as possible.

Zero rating has arisen in the United Kingdom largely for political reasons. It applies to items such as food and children's clothing. Again there is a list, and a golden rule. The rule is: anything which isn't listed as zero rated is

standard rated. Standard rating currently means VAT at 17.5 per cent.

The main danger to business again springs from classification. We don't want to treat a sale as zero rated only to find that the VATman later disagrees with us. The business could then be faced with the problem of trying to recover from customers the VAT that should have been charged. Even if that proves impossible, the VATman will still want a share of the money received on the sale. Overall it can be a very costly mistake.

Items which are zero rated are as follows:

- Food
- Sewerage and water services
- Books
- Talking books for the blind and handicapped, and wireless sets for the blind

- Construction of domestic housing
- Transport
- Caravans and houseboats
- Gold and bank notes
- Drugs, medicines and aids for the handicapped
- Certain clothing and footwear
- Certain items used by charities
- Certain items supplied in tax-free shops

We can sum zero rating up like this:

- Used to keep down cost to final consumer
- Applies to certain specified items
- Many zero-rated items are politically sensitive
- Some are seen as basic necessities
- Recent changes are eroding principle of zero rating
- Prime example of this is introduction of positive rate of VAT on heating fuel

Paying VAT

Now it's time to look at the next two VAT building blocks. These are paying VAT and reclaiming VAT.

VAT is designed as a tax on the final consumer. It is not intended as a tax on business. This is why the tax route from the real world to the government can become convoluted. A chain of businesses may get involved before the consumer gets his or her hands on the finished product. In theory, those businesses will be able to reclaim any VAT they have paid out in the process. So from a consumer point of view, VAT is always about paying. From a business point of view, it can be about making payments *and* getting refunds.

VAT now comes in two sizes: a standard rate of 17.5 per cent; a lower rate of 8 per cent. The 8 per cent rate applies to domestic fuel. The standard rate of 17.5 per cent applies to everything else, unless it is included in the list of exemptions, or is zero rated.

Consumers have to dig into their pockets to pay this VAT. Most things they buy are taxable, from paper to washing machines, from petrol to videos. Some items on the weekly shopping list are taxable too. These include cleaning materials, sweets, fizzy drinks and alcohol.

Standard rated VAT falls not just on goods like these. Services are also taxed. The solicitor's bill and the accountant's fee can include VAT. Mole-catchers, gorillagrams, and taxidermists can all charge VAT on their services. Almost everything is taxable.

Charging VAT

But while the law says that a wide range of goods and services are taxable, not all businesses can actually charge the tax. Only businesses which are registered with Customs and Excise can do so. Tomorrow we shall look at the process of VAT registration. For now, all we need to bear in mind is another Customs and Excise classification. This says that there are two types of business: those that are registered for VAT, and those that are not registered.

Getting VAT back

So if VAT is aimed at the consumer, rather than at business, how does it work? The theory is that each business charges tax only on the value it has added to the goods it processes. If it provides a service, then it is supposed to charge tax on the profits it makes in providing the service. In practice, this means that payments of VAT shuttle back and forth between the business world and Customs and Excise.

Put technically, the system runs on tax credits. Businesses which are registered for VAT charge tax on the total value of goods or services they sell. They then pay this across to the VATman.

However, VAT-registered businesses are entitled to make a deduction from the sum that they owe the VATman. This covers any VAT that they have themselves paid out for goods and services used to make their sales. For the VAT-registered gorillagram, for example, this means that the gorilla suit comes that bit cheaper. The VAT element included in the price of the suit can be deducted from the sum paid to Customs and Excise. The result of all this should, arithmetically, be equivalent to taxing only the added value.

Here is a checklist of points to give us an overview of the position.

The VAT cycle
- VAT is a tax on consumers rather than business
- Businesses collect tax on the 'value added' to their products
- Businesses pay this VAT to the VATman
- Businesses deduct from this the VAT they pay out

There are a number of variations on this theme:

- Businesses making zero rated supplies can reclaim VAT from VATman and usually get refunds
- Businesses making partly exempt and partly taxable supplies cannot reclaim all the VAT paid out
- Businesses not registered for VAT receive no refunds

The rules are different for VAT-registered businesses which make only zero-rated goods. These can reclaim the tax they pay, but they don't end up with tax to hand across to the VATman. For businesses like these, VAT is like a fruit machine that always pays out. It means refunds, refunds, refunds. Food retailers and farmers can often get refunds of VAT on a regular basis.

The rules are also different for hybrids: businesses which provide goods or services that are partly taxable and partly exempt. These businesses may be unable to reclaim all the tax that they pay on the goods and services they themselves use. Special calculations are required in these circumstances.

For businesses which are not registered for VAT, the question of refunds does not arise. They cannot recover any VAT they pay. These businesses have no dealings with the VAT man. They neither collect nor reclaim tax.

Usually only businesses can claim VAT back. Even charities are not allowed to do so, although there are some special rules designed to help charities, but these tend to apply only to specific items, for example, vehicles adapted for the use of wheelchairs. In general, the rules are designed to operate so that charities don't pay VAT in the first place.

Private individuals cannot register for VAT. In this way, the VATman aims to eliminate any possibility of subsidising hobby activities. But VAT would not be VAT if there weren't a few exceptions. In this case, there are special rules for private individuals to get back VAT if they build their own housing. We'll look at this on Thursday, along with other schemes.

Summary

Today we have looked at what VAT is paid, and when it is paid. The regime of VAT classifies all goods and services into three basic categories:

- Exempt supplies – no VAT charged to customers or claimed back
- Zero-rated supplies – VAT at zero per cent – business usually gets refunds
- Taxable supplies – positive rate of VAT charged to customers – business obtains a balance between VAT refunds and payments

Tomorrow we shall look at how businesses get into VAT – and out of it.

VAT registration

We know that businesses work for the VATman and collect VAT. Today we will look at how they get involved.

Getting in and out of VAT:
- The VAT-registered business
- Getting into VAT
- Getting out of VAT
- Special cases

Many of the businesses we come across are involved with VAT. We are going to look now at what that means: how a business gets into the VATman's web, and how it gets out. We shall also look at a few of the more unusual areas – the bits of the VAT web where the spider did overtime and made a few more special rules.

The VAT-registered business

The VAT-registered business is a tax collector. To show that it's an authorised tax collector, the VATman gives it a number. This VAT registration number is shown on all its till receipts and bills, and it is the VAT number which gives a business a place in the VAT cycle. The VAT-registered business has to comply with the letter of VAT law; it must classify what it sells so that the correct rate of tax is applied.

There are rules for what it buys too. Here it needs to know what VAT has been included in the price of any goods and services bought in.

The next part of the VAT cycle involves the registered business performing some calculations. The result of all the calculations is a return made to the central VAT office of Customs and Excise at Southend. This goes accompanied by a payment for the net tax collected, or a request for a refund.

VAT means hard work for business. More than that, for businesses that get VAT wrong, it can mean penalties. However, most businesses benefit positively from VAT and some actually choose to get involved in VAT, so it can't all be bad news!

Getting into VAT

Businesses can't always choose whether to register for VAT. There is no option in many cases. Registration is compulsory when business turnover goes over a certain limit. From 1 December 1993, the threshold is £45 000 per annum. We looked at sales which fall outside the scope of VAT yesterday. Such sales do not count towards this limit.

As many businesses exceed the £45 000 limit during the first year's trading, VAT is often part of the business equation from very early days.

Let's look now at the mechanics of getting registered. The first step is very easy: phone the local VAT office and ask for a registration form.

The VAT registration form

The registration form asks for a variety of details about the business which wants to register. The VATman will want to know who owns the business, and whether it is run as a company, a partnership or by a sole trader; where the business is based, and what it deals in; why the business wants to register, whether it uses a trading name and whether it uses a computer to keep its records. (There is also information about European Union sales and purchases to consider, and we'll look at the European dimension later in the week.)

Soon after the completed registration form arrives in the VATman's in-tray, the business will be sent its VAT number. This is the number that the business needs in order to charge VAT on its sales. A formal certificate of VAT registration arrives later. This certificate includes full details about registration and sets out the VAT trade classification. This describes the type of trade that the business is involved in. It also states the legal status of the business, and details of any special VAT schemes that the business may be going to use. It also gives details of which VAT office will be going to keep an eye on the business.

That's the straightforward scenario. But what happens if we're a more complicated case such as an entrepreneur with the proverbial finger in every pie?

The basic point we need to remember here is that VAT registration is meant to cover *all* the business activities being carried on by an individual, a partnership or a company.

If our enterprising gorillagram also makes motorway cones in his spare time, when he comes to register for VAT, there'll be VAT on everything: VAT on gorilla hugs and VAT on the motorway cones.

The VATman is vigilant in this area. There are special anti-avoidance provisions to keep businesses on the straight and narrow. If the gorillagram decides to put his motorway cone manufacturing under different ownership *just* to keep it out of VAT, the VATman will not be amused. In fact, he might well challenge the arrangement.

VAT registration options
You *must* register:

- If turnover in the last 12 months is over £45 000
- If you are organising a one-day event and expect your future turnover to be more than £45 000 in the next 30 days

You *may* register:

- If you are carrying on a business (rather than a hobby) and what you sell is taxable, even if turnover is below £45 000

You *may not* register:

- If you make only exempt sales

Getting out of VAT

The VATman only lets a business out of his clutches in certain circumstances. There are six main reasons why a business would cancel its VAT registration:

- It stops trading
- It registered for VAT before it started trading. For whatever reason, the venture is no longer going ahead
- The business is sold
- It changes the way it is run, for example, a change from a partnership to a company, or from a one-person business to a partnership
- Turnover falls, and it is likely that next year, turnover will be below £43 000 per annum (limit set 1.12.93)
- Sales are all – or nearly all – zero rated, and the business would usually get refunds if it carried on with VAT registration.

When a business falls into one of these categories, it's easy enough to cancel VAT registration; it only takes one form.

Special cases

VAT wouldn't be VAT if there weren't a few special cases.
Now that we've looked at how the system usually works,
it's time to look at a few variations.

- Businesses that can't register
- Businesses that ask not to register
- Companies in groups and divisions

Businesses that can't register
Businesses that sell only goods or services that are outside
the scope of VAT (exempt supplies) are in a special position.
If everything they sell is exempt, they can't register for VAT.
This means that they can't reclaim any of the VAT they have
to pay on goods and services they buy in.

If the sales are mixed – some exempt, some taxable – there
are different rules again. Here a business may be allowed to
register, but when it comes to calculating turnover in
relation to the VAT registration limit, the exempt sales don't
count. A business in this position can't reclaim *all* the VAT it
pays out, only part of it. In VAT-speak, this is called
apportionment. The VATman can give guidance on how to
do the calculations.

Businesses that ask not to register
A registered business that sells mostly zero-rated goods will
usually get VAT refunds. This is because there is no VAT to
charge on the goods it sells, but plenty to claim back on the

goods it buys in. To see how this works in practice, let's look at Farmer Giles.

Farmer Giles pays lots of VAT. He buys a tractor, gallons of fuel, new gates and fence posts, pays the vet's bill and auction mart charges. Bills, bills, bills, and there's VAT on most of them. But when it comes to Farmer Giles' sales, it's a different matter. No VAT on his livestock. It's zero rated. No VAT on the milk. It's zero rated. So by and large, Farmer Giles gets refunds, and there are special rules so that he can get them monthly.

All the same, businesses in circumstances like these may want nothing to do with VAT. They may feel, for example, that the size of the refunds they get doesn't do enough to compensate them for the time and effort they have to put in to VAT, keeping records and making returns.

This is where a business could ask to be exempted from registering for VAT. If a business produces only zero-rated goods, the VAT man is likely to agree. The same applies if a business can show that the VAT it could reclaim would normally be more than the VAT it would charge on its sales. If effect, businesses like these would not be collecting any VAT for the VATman. So he is likely to let them out of the system.

Companies in groups and divisions

Companies often have complicated structures. Many are arranged in groups with holding companies and subsidiaries, or in administrative divisions. VAT rules recognise this complexity. The normal VAT rule is that it is a legal entity – such as a single company – that registers for VAT. But for administrative reasons, the VAT man is prepared to accept a variation on this theme for companies organised in groups and divisions.

Group registration   Group registration works like this. One member of the group is nominated as the 'representative member'. It is then treated as receiving and selling to the outside world. Everything that the group buys in gets treated as the representative member's purchases. All sales are treated as its sales. The representative member also deals with Customs and Excise. It is the one to make VAT returns, pay the VAT man and so forth.

Transfers of goods and supplies of services inside the group are then ignored for VAT purposes. If the companies were not in a VAT group, this would not be the case. Instead each would need to charge VAT on transfers to other companies inside the group. Group registration is not automatic. It must be applied for. Customs and Excise then have to process and approve the application.

Divisional registration   Divisional registration is different. This type of VAT registration is appropriate for companies which are organised in divisions, each run as a separate business. With divisional registration, each division has its own VAT number. It prepares its own returns and accounts for its own VAT. The company acts as fall guy. If a division was to default on its VAT payment to Customs and Excise, the company would have to pick up the tab. Supplies made by one division to another do not count as taxable supplies. This means that the divisions don't charge VAT on these transactions.

Summary

Today we have looked at getting in and out of VAT, and what it means to do so. In both cases, it is a matter of filling in the correct application form. The forms themselves are quite straightforward. Once more, the real art is recognising the VAT man's categories.

We can sum up the VAT rules we have looked at today like this:

- Businesses must register for VAT if turnover is £45 000 p.a. or more
- Businesses may choose to register if annual turnover is less than this
- Implications of VAT registration:
  - Business gets registration number
  - Is authorised to collect VAT

- Has to classify sales
- Has to work out VAT on purchases
- Periodic day of reckoning with VAT man
- Businesses can deregister for VAT:
  - If turnover falls below limits
  - For other specified reasons

Cutting up the VAT cake

Now we have seen how businesses get into VAT and charge tax on their goods and services. New we shall look at how the VAT cake gets cut up when the VATman wants his share.

- The business slice: claiming VAT back on purchases
- The VATman's slice: paying VAT out on sales
- Working out payments and refunds
- When there's a dispute

Businesses playing the VAT game collect money from their customers and pay money out to their suppliers. But sooner or later, the VATman is going to want his share of the action. How does he cut into the cake and how do we work out how big a slice he gets?

VAT-registered businesses are required to keep their VAT separate from business money. This is done by keeping a record of the VAT received and the VAT paid out. Then, periodically, the VATman issues a special form – the VAT return. This is his invitation to carve up the cake.

How often the VATman does this is worked out very early on, when a business first registers for VAT. Customs and Excise gives the business a set of return periods. This means that for ever after, at the end of each return period, the VATman will pop a VAT return in the post. This will have to be completed and sent back before the end of the following month. Most businesses have a return period of three months. Some businesses get a return period of one month and find themselves formfilling every four weeks!

To complete a VAT return, a business has to do a calculation. This establishes the total VAT received and the total VAT paid out. The difference is the VATman's share, or, in some cases, the slice he's going to give back to the business.

All this is straightforward. But not all VAT is the same. Sometimes not all the VAT that has been paid out can be claimed back. Sometimes a business is deemed to have sold goods to itself. In this way, various rules and regulations affect the size of the business slice of VAT cake, and the size of the VATman's slice.

The business slice: claiming VAT back on purchases

The business slice of the VAT cake is what a business can claim back. What it can claim back depends on what it sells.

This may seem a strange way of looking at things, but the real principle behind it is this: were the items used to make taxable sales? This is called the attribution principle. It is the first restriction on claiming back VAT.

What can a business claim back?
VAT can only be reclaimed on items used to make taxable supplies. If a business produces exempt goods, it can't usually recover the VAT on items purchased to make them. It also means that some overhead expenses could be contentious. This is because they may not be directly related to sales. Beyond this rule, there are specific items of expenditure which do not qualify.

Businesses run as partnerships or by sole traders may also have to think about what they claim back in order to make allowances for any element of private use. They may have, for example, shared business and domestic costs.

The gorillagram working out of his front room at home may have to think hard about what he does with the bill when the house needs rewiring. Special rules also apply to cars. The VATman will accept adjustments made on any 'just and reasonable' basis.

There may be other adjustments that a business needs to make to what it can claim back. The biggest category is the special calculations required when a business is on a VAT scheme of one kind or another.

We have seen that it may not be possible to claim back all the VAT that has been paid out on purchases. So, throwing to one side all the bills on which we can't claim back VAT, what happens next? We add up all the VAT we've paid to suppliers. We subtract any element for private use. We do any special scheme calculations. We're left with a figure at the end of all these steps, which is the maximum VAT we can claim back.

The VATman's slice: paying VAT out on sales

Working out the VATman's slice is in principle very simple. All the tax a business collects on its sales is payable to Customs and Excise. The business knows what rate of tax to charge. The customer has been sent a bill. The business adds up the VAT and pays it over, pausing only to subtract the VAT it has paid to suppliers.

Can it really be that easy? Yes, sometimes it is, but not always. There may be a few complications and problem areas:

- Customer complications
- Operational complications
- Selling to yourself
- Private use of business assets

Customer complications
Discounts   VAT is normally calculated on the net selling price, after taking off the discount.

Trade-ins   For any part exchange, VAT must be based on the full market value, for both halves of the deal. It is not charged on the net settlement figure.

Sale or return   This is fine for 12 months, but if the customer hasn't made up his mind to buy by then, VAT must be paid as if sold.

Foreign currency   A basis is agreed with the local VAT office. Alternatively, the exchange rates issued by Customs and Excise can be used. The rate of exchange for the date of supply is the one to use: not the exchange rate at the date of settlement.

Bad debts   Automatic relief after 12 months when the debt is written off in the accounts.

Operational complications
Don't think about charging VAT here:

- Business gifts under £10
- Free meals to employees
- Staff tips
- Postage in mail order business
- Business sold as going concern

On the other hand, the following are subject to VAT:

- Occasional postal transactions
- Sale of business and assets piecemeal

Selling to yourself

The VATman has invented the concept of selling to yourself. He has good reasons for this. If a business prints its own stationery, builds its own factory, or makes its own cars, then somewhere along the line, the VATman may lose out. If the business had gone out and bought on the open market, the VATman would probably have ended up with a bigger slice of the action. This applies particularly in the case of businesses that make some exempt sales and so can't claim back all the VAT they pay to suppliers. Never one to pass up an opportunity, the VATman worked out a few rules to sort this one out. Consider the following scenario. Spendthrift and Scrooge run a casino.

Betting and games of chance are exempt from VAT, but Spendthrift and Scrooge also have a bar selling taxable beer, wine and spirits. They want to print new letterheads and provide pre-printed writing paper and envelopes so their

customers can more easily write begging letters when they run out of funds. So they ask a local printer out one evening, and send their staff round to the printer's to do a spot of work. Back they come with the letterheads and paper. Not an episode the VATman is happy with at all. If the printer had done the work, Spendthrift and Scrooge would have had to pay VAT, but they wouldn't have been able to claim it all back.

This is where the concept of selling to yourself comes in. Spendthrift and Scrooge are treated as though they had sold the paper to themselves. So Spendthrift and Scrooge become both supplier and customer. As the supplier, they charge VAT on the paper and labour costs. As the customer, they have to pay VAT. If they could claim back all the VAT they pay as the customer, the two sides would cancel out, and the VATman would still be empty-handed, but because some of Spendthrift and Scrooge's supplies are exempt, they can't claim back all the VAT; their claim is restricted.

So as far as Spendthrift and Scrooge are concerned, printing their own stationery turns into something of an own goal: Spendthrift and Scrooge 1, Customs and Excise 2.

This situation doesn't apply to many businesses. But for businesses in the exempt sales sector, such as financial services and insurance, it can cause problems.

Private use of business assets

This is a problem area that many of us are likely to come across. Cars are the prime example. What happens when a business pays for fuel for cars which are used not only for work, but also for private trips? The answer is – the VATman comes along for the ride!

Cars with business and private use
- Private use treated as sale of fuel by business to employee/business owner
- Business must therefore pay a pre-set scale charge
- Scale charge reduced for high business mileage
- Scale charge not affected by private mileage total

Working out payments and refunds

To work out payments and refunds of VAT, we draw together the different areas we have looked at today:

First the business works out what it owes the VATman. Then it works out what it can claim back. Then it subtracts one total from the other. These total figures go on the VAT return. If the business has collected more VAT than it has paid out, it pays the VATman; it has to share its cake with the VATman. If it has paid out more VAT than it's collected, it gets a refund, so that VATman has to share some of his cake.

From time to time the VATman checks the calculations and adjustments that make up the figures on the VAT return. We'll look at this detail on Saturday. For now, we'll just note that a business and the VATman may sometimes disagree. What happens then? We'll look at this next.

When there's a dispute

Is a 300-metre journey down a mineshaft travel? Should worms you feed to fish be counted as purchases? Can a school tuck-shop become a business? Are royal-jelly capsules food? These are the sort of areas that can cause dispute – areas of subtle VAT distinctions.

A business that can't reach an agreement with the VATman can take questions like these to an appeal body: the VAT tribunal. Its answers to the questions above are: no, yes, yes, no. In fact, it went so far as to say that royal jelly capsules don't look, taste, or fill the stomach like food. So there we

are. Questions and rulings like these give us some idea of the very precise way in which the VATman oversees his world.

These are the guidelines to bear in mind when dealing with tricky areas:

- Ask Customs and Excise for advice as soon as possible
- Get an opinion in writing as individual VAT officers may give different opinions of the same issue
- If all else fails, consider an independent review by a VAT tribunal

Summary

Today we have seen how to work out VAT payments and refunds, in order to cut up the VAT cake. We can sum up like this:

- Business owes VATman the total VAT collected on sales plus possible extras such as any VAT on sales to yourself, VAT on fuel scale charges, VAT on sales of business assets etc.
- Business can claim back from VATman any VAT paid to suppliers
- Adjustments may be needed for private use of business assets and items used to make exempt supplies
- In case of dispute, get VATman's opinion in writing. If all else fails, go to VAT tribunal

Tomorrow we shall look at the paperwork involved.

The VAT paper trail

So far we have seen how businesses charge VAT to consumers and other businesses, collect money for the VATman, and claim back VAT. Now it's time to turn detective. Today we look at the VAT paper trail:

- Evidence for purchases
- Evidence for sales
- Tax points
- Certificates and more certificates

The VATman, heavily disguised as Inspector Barrel, is on the alert. He has heard that some unscrupulous operators are making false claims for repayment from Customs and Excise. The figures on their VAT returns have no basis in reality. He is also getting complaints that some firms are charging VAT although they are not entitled to do so. It's clearly time to check the paperwork.

Evidence for purchases

Barrel plans some inspection visits. He is going to start by looking at evidence for purchases. No false claims for repayment are going to get past him. First stop is Claim it Back Ltd. This is a newly formed company that has recently presented the VATman with a return showing a repayment claim of £1 million. Barrel is shown into a backroom with shelves of files labelled 'purchases'. Pulling down a file, Barrel sifts through the invoices.

Claim it Back seem to have paid out a lot of cash: the No Such Company £225 000, the Anything Goes Partnership £315 735. Barrel turns to page 41 of his *VAT Guide* – 'Information required on a VAT invoice'.

Invoices are the next step in the VAT paper trail. To qualify as a VAT invoice, an invoice must give certain details. Checking the invoices collected by Claim it Back, Barrel notices that many necessary details are lacking. There will be no repayment for Claim it Back until the paperwork is properly sorted out.

An invoice Barrel doesn't like:

The Anything Goes Partnership
Charge for Claim it Back Ltd £315 735

Barrel's corrected version of the invoice:

G. & P.Z. STRANGEWAY T/A
The Anything Goes Partnership
305 Wellington Street
Blanchetown

VAT Registration No.
GB 735 555 555

Invoice No. 7171
Tax point: 17.7.94

Invoiced to:
Claim It Back Ltd
27 Marlborough Court
Bonepartville

To: sale of two new Alfapha jet dyeing machines, serial number 8157322/8179343 complete with synchronised timing systems

	269 715
VAT at 17.5%	46 020.12
	£ 315 735.12

Payment terms: 2.5% may be deducted for payment within 14 days. Otherwise strictly net.

N.B. VAT is correctly based on the discounted price of £269 715 less $2^{1}/_{2}\%$. viz 262972.12 x $17^{1}/_{2}\%$ = 46 020.12

Here is a checklist for a full VAT invoice:

- Name and address of supplier
- Name and address of customer
- VAT registration number of supplier
- Invoice serial number
- Tax point
- Description of goods or services supplied
- VAT rate
- VAT charged
- Note of discounts where relevant

Evidence for sales

Evidence for sales forms the next step in the paper trail.
Sales and purchases are the opposite sides of the same coin.
One business's sales are another business's purchases. We
can sum up what Barrel is looking for like this:

- Retail business (small sales) – till rolls
- Cash and carry wholesalers – till rolls, product code list
- Other sales – copy sales invoices

Even in retail sales, a tax invoice must be provided if a customer asks for one. For small sales, it can be a little less detailed than the full VAT invoices we looked at earlier, but there are still rules to comply with. Abbreviated VAT invoices for small retail sales should show:

- Supplier's name and address
- Supplier's VAT registration number
- Description of goods
- Rate of VAT
- Total charged included VAT
- For use only for sales under £100 (including VAT)

Dr Ambiguous, Managing Director of Anything Goes has a scheme that Barrel doesn't like the look of. She says it saves VAT on sales. It goes like this: Anything Goes is liable to pay VAT to Customs and Excise on the basis of its sales invoices. Each sales invoice clocks up a VAT liability. So Dr Ambiguous plans to cut the paper trail completely. If Anything Goes don't raise any sales invoices . . . they don't pay any VAT. Right?

Wrong. Barrel waves his blue VAT book in the air. This is where he proves that Customs and Excise has thought of everything. There are rules about paying VAT where there's no paperwork. No degree of capering off the paper trail can take a business out of the VAT man's clutches. VAT is a tax like an octopus. It has very long tentacles.

So how does the long arm of VAT work here? How does a supplier become liable to pay VAT to Customs and Excise even if there's no paperwork? Tax points are the answer.

Tax points

Tax points are dates. There are many different types of tax point; basic tax points, actual tax points, continuous sales tax points, adoption of goods, goods in the possession of the buyer. However, all we need to note here is simply that a VAT-registered business starts running up a liability to the VATman once the tax point is passed. This is the case whether or not the business is sticking to the VAT paper trail and issuing the right invoices.

Basic tax points

The basic tax point is the date when goods are sent to a customer – or are collected – or are first made available to a customer. For businesses which sell a service, the basic tax point is the date when all work has been carried out, and there's only the invoicing still to go.

The VATman can resort to the basic tax point if no paperwork is raised, or if no payment is made.

> *Basic tax points:*
> * When goods sent to customer
> * When service complete and only invoice outstanding

But the basic tax point is not used in every case. It can be overridden in a variety of circumstances. A different tax point, such as an actual tax point is then used instead.

Actual tax points

An actual tax point replaces the basic tax point where money is received, or an invoice issued before the goods are physically transferred from seller to buyer. The actual tax point here is the earlier date; the date that money is received or an invoice issued.

Let's look at an example:

> * Gay Paris Ltd makes model Eiffel Towers
> * Sends model to customer 14 February
> * Gets paid 10 February
> * Actual tax point 10 February

Where a supplier raises an invoice within 14 days of the transfer of goods, an actual tax point can also be used instead of the basic tax point. Here the invoice date would replace the date of supply as the tax point. It works like this:

- Gay Paris Ltd sends model to customer 14 February
- Raises invoice 17 February
- Actual tax point 17 February

As far as invoicing is concerned, using the basic tax point, there are 30 days to raise an invoice. The tax point would then be the date of the supply. It is possible to make an extension to this timetable, but this would have to be agreed with the VATman.

So the long arm of the VATman is very long indeed, and a business can't get out of its obligation to pay VAT to Customs and Excise by failing to raise invoices.

Inspector Barrel is still waving his blue VAT book in the air, having clinched his point. For a practical demonstration, he walks across the office to the drinks machine. He inserts two coins, presses the button and collects an ice-cold can of fizz. 'And what', he asks Dr Ambiguous, 'Do you do about this?'

Now that we've got to grips with the concept of tax points, we know what Barrel is driving at. A basic tax point has just taken place. Every time the drinks machine makes a sale, there is a tax point. Goods have been transferred from seller to buyer. There's no paperwork – so we assume a basic tax point. From a practical point of view, the date when the cash is emptied from the machine would be accepted as the tax point.

Certificates and more certificates

The VAT paper trail is almost complete. But there's one more class of paperwork still to look at today. VAT certificates. For not only are there papers generated by the purchases and sales of a business included in the trail, there are also records generated by Customs and Excise; in particular, VAT certificates.

A VAT registration certificate is held by all VAT-registered businesses and is very important as it guarantees the seller's right to charge VAT. A VAT scheme certificate confirms scheme membership and is the key to interpreting other business records.

Summary

Today we have followed the VAT paper trail. We have followed through the maze of registration numbers, VAT invoices and VAT certificates.

The VAT paper trail:
- Correct paperwork critical to VATman
- Problems for businesses with incorrect paperwork
- Possibility of penalties
- VAT due even in absence of paperwork
- Paper trail starts with VAT registration number and registration certificate
- Registration number follows through on to VAT invoices for sales and purchases
- Valid VAT invoices for sales and purchases follow specified format

Schemes and exceptions

So far, we have looked at how VAT usually works, and we have seen something of the basic rules. However, there are always exceptions and today we will look at how the basic rules are applied or modified in various cases.

- Schemes for smaller businesses
- Schemes for trades
- Special cases

Bending the rules

Because of its comprehensive scope, VAT can affect entirely different types of activity and entirely different types of business. Multinational businesses and corner shops, *haute couturiers* and steeplejacks alike feel its impact, but the impact may not be the same for each business. Selling second-hand ponies is different from dealing in foreign currency, and the effect of VAT may be different too.

There are times when it would be unreasonable to treat all
businesses in the same way, and the VATman recognises
this. This is where VAT schemes come in. They mean that in
a world of round holes, the VATman is trying to help the
square pegs.

Help from the VATman
We can sum up the aim of VAT schemes like this:

- Rescue the odd man out
- Make VAT more equitable in its impact
- Iron out problems in applying VAT rules
- Make life easier for businesses
- Cater for specific types of business

The VATman also tries to cater for businesses that have
round-hole and square-peg problems by issuing guidance
on difficult and contentious areas. Listed below are some of
the background information notices available from the
VATman:

- *VAT Publications*
- *VAT Enquiries Guide: How to Get Information from
  Customs and Excise*
- *Filling in Your VAT Return*
- *Keeping Records and Accounts*
- *The VAT Guide*

Schemes for smaller businesses

Cash flow is the life blood of business. For smaller businesses, even little hiccoughs in cash flow can be disastrous. The first scheme we are going to look at today is one designed to help cash flow in the smaller business. For this purpose, a small business is defined by the VATman as a business whose annual turnover is up to £350 000. Businesses with a turnover greater than this are not allowed to join the scheme. For businesses whose turnover fits the bill, membership is optional. The scheme is called the cash accounting scheme. Here's an overview:

Cash accounting scheme:
- Turnover below £350 000 p.a.
- Account to VATman only when paid for sales
- Optional scheme
- Helps cash flow

Other businesses:
- Any level of turnover
- Account to VATman when tax point passed

To grasp the significance of the cash accounting scheme, we need to look back to the normal VAT rules about collecting and paying tax. Remember tax points? We looked at these yesterday. The basic tax point is the date that goods are sent to a customer, or the date that services are completed. This is the date that sets the VAT clock ticking. From this date, the business that is making the sale is liable to account to

Customs and Excise for the VAT on the sale. It doesn't matter whether the customer has paid up at this stage: any VAT due on the sale must be included on the next VAT return.

A problem of cash flow

Let's look at how this works in practice. Here's Mr Phixit, a plumber. He has recently installed a new central heating system for International Business Plc at their offices in Foxbridge. His bill comes to £20 000 plus VAT of £3 500, a grand total of £23 500.

Mr Phixit sends the bill to International Business Plc at their accounts department on 28 March. His VAT return period ends on 30 April. Has he got paid by this time? No. He rings the accounts department on 29 April and asks why the bill is outstanding. They say that the account has been sent to Foxbridge for verification. They will be happy to release their cheque – but only after the verification from Foxbridge has been received – and that may take a month.

Under normal VAT rules, Mr Phixit would have to include the £3 500 VAT in the VAT he owes to Customs and Excise on the VAT return to 30 April. However many excuses International Business come up with, regardless of the fact that his bill might not get paid for three or four months, this would be the VAT timeable. In terms of cash flow, having to pay the VAT across before he gets paid could produce more of a terminal gasp than a minor hiccough.

The rules of the cash accounting scheme come to the rescue here. The cash accounting scheme allows Mr Phixit to ignore the date of the bill he sends out. Instead he can wait until he actually gets paid before he has to account to the VATman for the VAT on his sale. Faced with the choice of joining the cash accounting scheme or pawning his grandmother, Mr Phixit decides to join the cash accounting scheme.

The cash accounting scheme can be beneficial in circumstances like Mr Phixit's. Essentially it can be useful for businesses which have fairly large sums owing to them at any one time, and which find that their customers are slow to pay.

But there is rarely something for nothing in business. With the cash accounting scheme there is a quid pro quo. Joining the scheme means a business makes the VATman wait for his money until it gets paid. So he makes the business wait too. It has to wait longer before it can reclaim the VAT charged by its suppliers. Businesses in the cash accounting scheme have their own timetable for reclaiming VAT. They can only do so when they have actually paid their bills. Under normal VAT rules, VAT could be reclaimed as soon as a VAT invoice was received.

Annual accounting scheme

Another scheme designed to assist the smaller business is the annual accounting scheme. Here is an overview:

> *Annual accounting scheme:*
> - Turnover up to £300 000 p.a. to qualify
> - Business must be registered for VAT for a minimum of 12 months before joining
> - One VAT return p.a. only to complete
> - Optional scheme
> - Intended to cut administrative burden

So far we have seen a variety of schemes planned by the VATman to help small businesses across the busy road of VAT. Although not their exclusive domain, smaller businesses may also be helped by retail- and trade-specific schemes. We shall look at these next.

Schemes for trades

There is a whole range of trade-specific schemes. These include schemes for tour operators, antique dealers, farmers and retailers. There is also a host of schemes for what are classed as second-hand goods – from ponies to cars and from electronic organs to aircraft.

Retail schemes
Let's look first at retail schemes. This is perhaps the most important group of all. The schemes are designed to cope with the very practical problems that retailers can face in trying to untangle the VAT element of the money they take.

Practical problems at point of sale:
- How to classify sales – exempt, zero or standard rated?
- Does sales price include VAT?
- How much VAT is included in sales price?

To appreciate exactly what a VAT-registered retailer is up against, we'll try a practical example.

A retail headache
We have agreed to help a friend out. She runs a chain of minimarkets. Can we hold the fort one Saturday morning? They're short staffed . . .

We're at the checkout. Here come the customers. The first clutches a bag of salt. What about salt and VAT? We reach for the *VAT Guide*. It seems that there are different sorts of salt. Different types of salt get different VAT treatment. So is this dendritic salt, or granular salt? The label leaves us none the wiser.

Meanwhile, there's another customer in the queue. We can see he's sporting some frozen yoghurt. VAT and yoghurt – an alarm bell rings in our minds. Is this what the VATman would classify as 'frozen yoghurt of a type you can't eat with a spoon from frozen'? How can we tell? By whipping a spoon out from behind the cash register and asking to try some?

As if this isn't enough of a problem, we can just about see customer number three. He's waving a packet of betel leaves in one hand and a box of paper clips in the other.

How on earth can we possibly know if the prices we are cheerfully ringing up on the till include VAT? How can we sort it all out at the point of sale? Retail schemes are there to help. They are named alphabetically, from A to J. Each scheme represents a different way of sorting out the VAT element in sales. Retailers who are able to isolate the VAT element at the point of sale can use Scheme A. Those who can't are given a variety of choices from Scheme B to J.

Scheme A
- For retailers who can isolate VAT at point of sale

Schemes B to J
- For retailers who can't isolate VAT at point of sale
- Use different methods to estimate VAT element in sales
- Some use purchase to sales ratios
- Some use estimated selling margin

Second-hand goods schemes

There are also special schemes for businesses that deal in second-hand goods. Under normal VAT rules, the dealer buys in his stock, adds VAT to the price he wants to charge, and waits for a customer. With a second-hand goods scheme, he only has to charge VAT on the profit margin. Second-hand schemes operate in the following areas:

- Cars
- Motorbikes
- Caravans and motorcaravans
- Boats and outboard motors
- Aircraft
- Electronic organs
- Firearms
- Horses and ponies
- Works of art, antiques and collectibles

Special cases

Here we will focus on two schemes; the DIY builder scheme and the capital goods scheme.

DIY builder scheme
This scheme aims to create a level playing pitch. It irons out the difference between people buying a new house from commercial builders, and private individuals who set out to build their own new housing. We have to bear in mind that new residential housing is zero rated for VAT.

Under the VAT DIY scheme, members of the public are allowed to claim back the VAT they pay out. Under normal VAT rules only VAT-registered businesses could do this.

Capital goods scheme
As we saw on Monday, a trader who makes exempt supplies can't claim all his or her VAT back. So what does the VATman do when a business that has been making taxable supplies and claiming back VAT in the usual way, starts to make some exempt supplies as well? He puts forward the capital goods scheme.

Capital goods scheme:
- For businesses making some taxable, some exempt supplies
- Affects treatment of VAT on certain capital purchases, e.g. computers, computer equipment, land and buildings of specified value (£50 000 computers; £250 000 buildings)
- Compulsory scheme

A fully taxable business can reclaim from the VATman all the VAT on the purchase of computers or buildings. A partially exempt business cannot. When a taxable business which has reclaimed VAT on computers or buildings in the past, starts to make exempt supplies, the VATman will ask for some of this VAT back. The capital goods scheme works out how much.

Summary

Tying together the strands we have looked at today, we can put all the elements together like this. The basic VAT rules are modified in some circumstances by VAT schemes and exceptions. These are designed to create a more level playing pitch. So to sum up:

- VAT schemes modify basic VAT rules
- Schemes help small business
- Schemes help specific trades
- Schemes help in special cases, e.g. DIY builders
- Schemes often have their own requirements for record keeping

VAT in Europe

Now we are ready to look beyond UK shores. VAT does not apply just to sales made in the UK. It is also an important tax in the European Union. We shall look at three main areas today:

- Europe, past, present and future
- Harmonising VAT across Europe
- European imports and exports now

Smugglers and the VATman don't mix. Policing imports and exports has always formed part of the Customs and Excise workload. But no VATman is an island. Now, more than ever before, UK VAT has to operate in a European framework. This is emerging only slowly. It reflects the legacy of past rules as well as the desire for an ever-closer union for the future. At present VAT in Europe is in a state of transition.

To work out where in the landscape of VAT we are, and why we've got there, we will look first at the role of VAT in Europe. Then we examine the EU's intentions for the future of VAT. Next we focus on how VAT used to operate across Europe. Putting the landmarks of future and past together brings us to VAT now: the reality of VAT in 1994.

Role of VAT in Europe
First of all – the 'why' of VAT in Europe. What is its function? VAT is a big European fund raiser. In 1970, the mandarins in Europe decided that the bulk of European Community (as it was then) revenue was going to come from one tax: VAT. They also decided that a proportion of the VAT collected in Member States would be channelled directly to Community funds. For these reasons, VAT is important socially and politically, as well as economically. So much for the theory. In practice, this means an intricate spider's web of law and procedure. The web is still being spun.

> *VAT in Europe:*
> - Provides EU revenue
> - Main source of funds
> - Detailed rules required
> - Law still in flux

Europe, past, present and future

Having come to terms with why VAT is important in Europe, we can now take a look at how the planners want their tax to work. Because VAT is a tax on sales, we must also take in the wider background, and look at the European ideal for trade. This ideal has important implications for VAT.

VAT time clock
The planners don't have a blank sheet of paper to write on. This is a key fact to bear in mind as we steer our way round the maze of VAT in Europe. The planners have specific aims for how VAT should work in future. They also have a whole new set of procedures to implement. But to get to the future, they have to alter the present, and this can't be done in one step. This means that they have to bring in an intermediate set of procedures in order to get to their ultimate goal – another set of procedures. Don't worry if it sounds a bit like going from A to B by way of C: you're quite right. It is. Intermediate procedures were set in place on 1 January 1993. These procedures allow the long-term aims to be introduced. The ultimate system is unlikely to be set in place before January 1997.

VAT in an ever-closer union

Eurocrats are intent on an ever-closer union. As far as VAT goes, that means greater standardisation, but there's a long road ahead.

Currently, individual countries set their own VAT rates. Although there are overall guidelines, the present system permits considerable local independence. Some countries in fact charge VAT at up to five different rates.

The power to fix VAT rates is jealously guarded by European countries. Political, social and fiscal motives underpin policy decisions. VAT can, for example, be used as a trade weapon. It has the capability to distort markets. Let's look at this possibility. What happens if we throw European markets open with VAT rates as they stand at present? Interesting – and unusual – results. Customers flock to buy goods from the countries with the lowest VAT rates. Consider the European greyhound market. Overnight, Irish greyhounds become a bargain: and all because of local VAT rates. The same happens to Belgian chocolates. The greyhound and chocolate markets promptly fall to pieces, and local VAT rates are to blame.

Casting an eye on perils like these, Eurocrats are pressing for long-term change. They are bent on greater conformity. This is to be achieved in two main stages. The first stage is the intermediate system introduced on 1 January 1993. The second is the system to come into force by about January 1997. This second system is based on the 'origin' principle. It is to be supported by the introduction of a pan-European VAT clearing house. We'll look at these long-term changes in a few moments. For now, we'll focus on the European trade ideal. This is the key to understanding why an intermediate set of VAT procedures was introduced. Or, to put it another way, why we have to go from A to B by way of C.

Trade: the European ideal

The EU is committed to free trade. It aims at a free trade zone stretching right across Europe. An important step towards this goal was taken on 1 January 1993. This was the date of the creation of the single European market; the abolition of fiscal frontiers within the EU.

The abolition meant that goods could move freely across Europe. The juggernauts no longer stop and disappear under a mountain of paperwork at ports and border-crossing points. Their drivers just keep moving.

As far as free trade goes, this is definitely a juggernaut in the right direction. The problem comes when the VATman tries to get in on the act.

Europe and trade:
- Aim – free trade zone
- Solution – remove fiscal frontiers
- Problem – VAT collection

Time was when the lorry-load of imports stopped for inspection. There was time to impound the goods, add on duties, charge VAT. What happens to the VATman when the lorry drives on by?

Free trade: a VAT collection headache
The European free trade policy, with its removal of fiscal frontiers, poses a VAT collection headache. Confronted by convoys of rapidly moving vehicles, how and when does the VATman collect his money?

The answer is that officials get together and devise a new operating system. In the long term, VAT will be collected on the origin principle. We mentioned this a little earlier. Essentially it means that in a trans-European deal, the VAT will be collected by the trader who sells the goods; and he will collect it in the country in which he is based. In effect it will be the origin of the trader that determines where VAT is collected. However, past procedures have to be adapted in order to move to this system.

UK VAT on European deals in the past
Customs and Excise has traditionally charged excise duties and VAT on goods imported to the UK. Exports also came under the VATman's scrutiny. We can sum the past position up like this:

Imports to UK:
- Charged to VAT in UK
- Treated like UK goods
- VAT due at point of entry to UK

Exports from UK:
- Not usually charged to VAT in UK

The aim of past UK policy was to treat imports in the same way as goods made and sold in the UK. VAT on imports was charged at the same rate as VAT on goods made and sold in the UK. The same classifications were used. This policy was intended to ensure that imports were not dramatically cheaper than home-produced goods.

A similar logic was applied to exports. The aim here was to make sure that goods made in the UK were not at a disadvantage in European markets. For this reason, exports were usually zero rated, whatever the goods involved. This tactic helped to keep the price of UK exports buoyant abroad. It also avoided the possibility of double taxation: tax in the UK and tax overseas.

We can see from this how the VAT treatment of imports and exports has political and economic implications. If we also note that the VAT involved was due at the point of entry to the UK, we are ready to summarise and move on. Here is a summary of the points we have looked at so far:

Europe aims for:
- Greater standardisation
- Free trade

Free trade leads to:
- Abolition of fiscal frontiers
- VAT collection problem

VAT on Euro deals:
- Formerly collected at point of entry to UK
- In long term collected on origin principle
- Currently on transitional system

The next step to understanding VAT in Europe is to look in greater detail at the move to harmonise VAT across Europe.

Harmonising VAT across Europe

The long-term VAT horizon includes the origin principle and the pan-European VAT clearing house. These will help harmonise VAT across Europe. It is time to add a bit more detail to the picture. We shall also look at two big obstacles standing in the way of efforts to harmonise VAT. They are regional variation in VAT rates and the problem of reclaiming VAT on purchases.

The origin principle
Using the origin principle to collect VAT means that the location of the seller is critical, as it is in this country that VAT will be collected.

Let's look at what this will mean for goods exported from the UK. Under the old system, British exports were usually zero rated, as we have already seen, but with the origin principle, things change. Sales to the EU would be treated just like sales within the UK. If VAT had to be charged to United Kingdom customers, it would be charged to EU customers too. This would effectively mean that the seller took no notice of to whom he was selling. There would be no difference between home sales and EU sales in this respect. The use of the origin principle represents a big step forwards in harmonising VAT across Europe.

But the origin principle lies in the future. It is unlikely to be used until January 1997. This is because of local variation in VAT rates and the problem of reclaiming VAT on purchases.

The origin principle:
- VAT collected in country where seller based
- Same treatment for UK home sales and EU sales
- Earliest date for introduction 1997
- Problems prevent earlier introduction

VAT rates

We have seen that at present, countries in the EU set their own rates of VAT. The guidelines state that the standard rate of VAT should not be less than 15 per cent. There are also reduced rates of VAT, which should not be charged at less than five per cent. In fact, the rates of VAT charged vary considerably. Standard rates of VAT vary from 15 per cent to 25 per cent. Reduced rates range from nought per cent to 12.5 per cent. To add to the confusion, Portugal also has a higher rate of VAT. This is charged at 30 per cent.

The Eurocrats' response to this is not to shout 'vive la difference'. They are looking for further harmonisation of VAT rates. The next date set for this is 1 January 1997.

Harmonisation of VAT is particularly important in a free trade environment. It is also vital for the introduction of the origin principle. At present, different EU countries charge different rates of tax on the same goods. A simple switch to the new system now would distort the markets. Customers could simply buy their goods in the countries with the lowest rate of VAT.

Reclaiming VAT on purchases
A second obstacle to the introduction of the origin principle is that of reclaiming VAT on purchases. As traders buy and sell across Europe, which government are they going to reclaim their VAT from?

The refund problem: a UK company, registered for VAT in UK, buys model Eiffel Towers from France. Under the origin principle, VAT is collected by the French seller and VAT on the purchase is reclaimed from the UK VATman in the usual way. The UK government then refunds the VAT.

The French company collects the VAT on the sale of model Eiffel Towers and accounts for the VAT to the French VATman in the usual way. The French government receives the VAT.

Here we can see that the French government ends up better off, but the UK government has to refund VAT it has never received. Applying the origin principle then, potentially means that governments of exporting countries would gain revenue. Governments of importing countries would lose revenue.

This is where a pan-European VAT clearing house comes in. The clearing house would settle the score between governments. In our example, the French government would reimburse the UK government for the VAT claimed back by the UK company. However, this solution is some years away, so at present we are in transition.

European imports and exports now

The creation of the single European market, with the abolition of fiscal frontiers on 1 January 1993, meant the introduction of transitional VAT collection procedures. Here is an overview.

From 1 January 1993:
- VAT on imports no longer due at point of entry
- Importing country takes VAT collection role
- New category of VAT registration introduced
- New lay-out of VAT return
- New returns of statistical data required

Imports
With the abolition of fiscal frontiers, the job of collecting VAT on imports passed to the business world. The VAT due on goods imported to the United Kingdom is payable by the company purchasing them. In effect, businesses buying goods from European Union countries have become import-agents for the VATman. To reflect this new role, a new category of VAT registration has been devised. This new registration is for businesses which buy goods from other EU countries. Such businesses may be required to register with the VATman so that they can account for VAT on the

goods they import. There have also been changes to VAT paperwork to accommodate the new procedures.

Additions to VAT paper trail:
- New VAT return lay-out for all traders
  - separate boxes for EU acquisitions
  - boxes completed only by traders importing goods
  - also requires statistical date on EU sales
- New forms for some traders
  - intrastat and EU sales listing
  - completed by firms trading with other EU Member States
  - some smaller firms exempted from completing these forms

Exports

Exports are the other side of the coin. There are two aspects to consider: exports to VAT-registered businesses and exports to non-VAT-registered businesses. Exports to VAT-registered businesses work like this:

Exports by one VAT-registered business to another:
- Goods despatched
- Supplier does not charge VAT
- Buyer liable to VAT in own country on delivery
- Buyer pays VAT at rate current in own country

With this scenario, the supplier is allowed to zero-rate the goods being exported. This means that he does not charge VAT, but there are important rules to follow here:

- Documentary proof of export required
- Seller's VAT number required on sales invoice
- Buyer's VAT number required on sales invoice

Fulfilling these conditions is critical. Exports to non-VAT-registered businesses work differently:

Exports by UK VAT-registered business to EU non-VAT-registered business:
- Goods despatched
- Supplier charges VAT in UK
- VAT charged at UK rates
- Buyer unable to reclaim any VAT paid

With this scenario, the purchaser is being taxed by a foreign government. This is not a state of affairs smiled upon by European politicians. There is again, the possibility of problems with local VAT rates. Individual customers might be able to buy goods at different prices in different countries, just because of the rate of VAT charged. It's the greyhound and chocolate problem all over again.

The VATman has come up with another new concept to cope with this last problem. This involves businesses registering for VAT in different European countries. It works like this:

- UK retailer sells talking clocks
- Sells to private customers in Belgium, not to business customers
- Goods manufactured and despatched from UK
- UK retailer required to register for VAT in Belgium if sales volume exceeds registration limit set by Belgian government
- Belgian VAT then charged on talking clocks sold to Belgian customers

This type of selling is called distance selling. Distance selling involves selling to private customers in a different country. If a company's business involves selling goods to private customers abroad, it may have to register for VAT with an overseas government just because of those sales. Each government can set its own registration limit for such sales. In the UK, the registration limit is £70 000. If a foreign company does business in excess of this limit, it has to register for UK VAT.

Summary

We have now looked at an outline of VAT in Europe. The rules are in a state of flux, and further change will be introduced in 1997. At present, transitional collection arrangements affect European imports and exports, and special rules apply to areas that Excise men have always taken to heart: wines, beers, spirits, tobacco etc.

We can sum up the European dimension to VAT like this:

- Aim – future VAT harmony
- Problem – existing VAT procedures
- Solution – interim procedures from 1.1.93
- Interim procedures allow aim of long-term procedures to be established, circa January 1997

The relationship with Customs and Excise

Now we have got a grip on the ins and outs of VAT, it is time to put the relationship with Customs and Excise under the microscope.

- Keeping records
- Inspection visits
- Penalties
- Summarising VAT : VAT returns

The relationship with the VATman is based on the 'Big Brother is watching you' principle. The VAT-registered business is collecting someone else's money: the VATman's. Come the day of reckoning at the end of each VAT accounting period, the VATman is waiting in the shadows. He is more than a little interested in whether the business gets its sums right, and as we have seen in earlier chapters, he has rules for everything. Businesses collect VAT on sales and recover VAT paid out on business purchases. The VAT authorities need to know that the amounts paid to them, and the refunds claimed from them, are correct.

They police the system in a variety of ways: they insist that businesses keep records; they send officers to inspect them: they charge penalties when businesses get it wrong; and they expect returns of income and expenses to be made each quarter.

Keeping records

The law demands that VAT-registered traders keep records, and Customs and Excise have powers to make detailed rules about what records are required. Many VAT-registered businesses will keep such records for a whole range of other reasons, but there are some records which are specific to VAT.

VAT records include all the normal paraphernalia of accounting records, and go beyond them. One particular addition is the VAT account. This is a quarterly summary of what the business owes to Customs and Excise, or what they owe the business. It shows how VAT shown in the accounting records has been dealt with, and discloses any adjustments made.

Some businesses have special VAT records because of the nature of their trade. Dealing in second-hand goods, for example, may mean joining a special VAT scheme. VAT schemes like this require special records.

The purpose of any VAT record is to keep a track on VAT coming into the business and VAT being paid out. Records are designed so that the business can charge the right amount of tax to customers and tell how much VAT has been charged by suppliers. This in turn allows the business to identify any adjustments that need to be made. Then the correct amount of VAT can be paid across to Customs and Excise. Alternatively, the right repayment can be requested.

To do all this, the records have to provide the right level of information about whatever is bought and sold. VAT records can be kept on computer or prepared manually. Whatever form they take, they have to be kept for six years.

At any time during this period, the VATman may step out of the shadows and announce that he would like to come and inspect them.

Inspection visits

Inspection visits are a daily part of the VATman's life. Your phone rings and you find yourself talking to someone who wants to come and look in at your business premises. An appointment is made. What happens when the big day dawns?

The primary interest is in the records, but the visit goes further than that. Usually the inspector will want to meet the chiefs and the Indians – senior staff with overall financial responsibility and staff involved in the day-to-day VAT recording. He may also want to get a feel for the business: touring the premises, looking at products, building up a picture of a day in the life of your business – these may all fit the agenda.

How often a business is likely to come face to face with a
VATman depends on all sorts of things. Any business that
registers for VAT can expect to be visited at least once in the
first three years. In general, the more complex the business,
the more frequent the visits. The greater the number of VAT
problems discovered, the more likely the performance is to
be repeated – and soon.

VATmen don't usually hunt in packs, and you are unlikely
to be confronted by more than one officer at a time.
Occasionally there may be a follow-up visit by a more senior
VATman who wants to review the work of a more junior
VATman. Remember that the whole system is one of checks
and double checks – magnifying glasses and bigger
magnifying glasses.

When a business goes under the magnifying glass at an
inspection visit, errors may come to light. Errors resulting in
VAT being underpaid, or repayments being overstated may
lead to penalties. Alternatively, errors resulting in VAT
being overpaid can be corrected and a refund made.

But however big the magnifying glass, it may not be big enough. If there are problems with VAT, a VAT visit can't find them all. That's not what it's designed to do. A visit can't give a clean bill of health. There may still be bugs in the system. It is always up to the business to find and disclose any errors there may be.

What is an inspector looking for?
- Errors in VAT returns
- VAT rules misinterpreted
- Sales classified wrongly
- Income understated
- Inadequate records
- Repayment claims overstated
- Lack of documentation for input tax claimed

Penalties

With VAT there are penalties for almost everything, and usually interest on unpaid tax too.

The most common penalties are imposed for making errors on VAT returns, sending returns and payments in late, or failing to register at the right time. These are the preserve of misdeclaration penalties and default penalties.

The basic principle underlying the penalties is to encourage prompt and accurate handling of VAT. Most VAT penalties operate like parking tickets with one twist. The size of the fine increases with the value of the car: sports cars come off worse than bubble cars.

VAT penalties get larger depending on the size of the error and the number of times errors are made. The technical term of a fine that increases in accordance with the size of the mistake is a 'tax-geared' penalty.

But there is a way out: it is called voluntary disclosure. Voluntary disclosure is the only way to avoid penalties. Mistakes disclosed before Customs and Excise are in any way on the alert should not attract penalties. Disclosure must be made in writing.

If a business discovers 'small' errors, these can usually be adjusted on the next VAT return. Small errors are defined as errors under £2 000. With these, there is no need to write to Customs and Excise. The adjustment made on the return is sufficient notice.

The system of penalties has not won many friends. Business-people have branded the system as unduly punitive, and c~ ·ive Chancellors of the Exchequer have tried to soften

After a wave of legislation designed to bring more businesses within the penalty net, the current trend is in the opposite direction. The March 1993 Budget introduced measures to make fewer businesses liable to penalties. Customs and Excise have announced that they will not necessarily impose a penalty in every case. A first offence for sending a VAT return and payment in late can be ignored. The spirit behind these relaxations differs sharply from earlier fire-breathing by Customs and Excise.

Other pitfalls:
- Tax evasion involving dishonest conduct
- Unauthorised issue of VAT invoices
- Late registration
- Any breach of rules

The Penalty Net

Summarising VAT: VAT returns

Here comes the chance to bring together everything covered so far – not just today, but this week – into one simple summary.

Understanding and handling VAT can be focused on one key piece of paper; the quarterly return that is usually called a 'VAT return'.

This is the document that gets sent to Customs and Excise Central Office in Southend. It tells the VATman how much VAT the business has collected and goes accompanied by a cheque. A business that is due a refund sends in a quarterly return and instead of posting a cheque, receives one.

Where do the figures on the return come from? There are basically four figures involved: for output tax, input tax, inputs and outputs.

Your total output tax
This is the VAT charged to customers on sales. To come up with this figure, remember to classify the sales.

Are they exempt – outside the scope of VAT? Or zero rated – taxed at nought per cent? Or standard rated – taxed at 17.5 per cent or 8 per cent? Remember to include any sales of equipment that have taken place, and to adjust for any non-business use of goods, equipment or vehicles.

Your total input tax
This is the VAT paid to suppliers on goods and services used in the business. Remember the principle of attribution. If the purchases cannot all be attributed to taxable sales, there will have to be an adjustment.

Total inputs
This is the value of goods and services acquired by the business in the period, excluding VAT.

Total outputs

This is the total value of sales made by the business in the period, excluding VAT.

If the business trades with other EU countries, the figures for tax due on imports and statistical totals for EU sales and purchases will have to be shown separately.

Armed with these figures any VAT return can be completed. However complicated a return may look, the sum is really simple:

> Total output tax less total input tax equals the amount owed to Customs and Excise. If the input tax figure is the larger, a refund is on its way.

The figures for inputs (total purchases) and outputs (total sales) are there for statistical purposes.

Summary

Now we can see how everything fits together:

- Keeping correct VAT records empowers business to:
  - complete VAT returns accurately
  - complete VAT returns on time
- Errors in returns may lead to penalties
- VAT returns constitute VATman's main source of information about a business
- VATman periodically checks returns against records

Looking at VAT records, returns, inspections and penalties today also helps to tie up all the VAT rules we have looked at this week:

Jargon
- Output tax – what a business charges to its customers
- Input tax – what a business is charged by suppliers
- Outputs – what the business sells
- Inputs – what the business buys

What's VAT?
- A tax on the final consumer
- Charged and collected by VAT-registered traders
- Cannot be charged by businesses not registered for VAT
- Administered by Customs and Excise
- Regulations for all occasions
- Not all types of goods and services taxable
- Businesses inspected for correct application of rules

The Business in a Week series

Doing Business in Europe in a Week
Finance for Non-Financial Managers in a Week
Introduction to Bookkeeping and Accounting in a Week
Succeeding at Interviews in a Week
Successful Appraisals in a Week
Successful Assertiveness in a Week
Successful Budgeting in a Week
Successful Business Writing in a Week
Successful Career Planning in a Week
Successful Computing for Business in a Week
Successful Customer Care in a Week
Successful Direct Mail in a Week
Successful Interviewing in a Week
Successful Leadership in a Week
Successful Market Research in a Week
Successful Marketing in a Week
Successful Meetings in a Week
Successful Mentoring in a Week
Successful Motivation in a Week
Successful Negotiating in a Week
Successful Presentation in a Week
Successful Project Management in a Week
Successful Purchasing in a Week
Successful Selling in a Week
Successful Stress Management in a Week
Successful Time Management in a Week
Successful Training in a Week
Understanding BPR in a Week
Understanding Just in Time in a Week
Understanding Quality Management Standards in a Week
Understanding Total Quality Management in a Week
Understanding VAT in a Week